ACKNOWLEDGEMENTS

These quotations were gathered lovingly but unscientifically over several years and/or were contributed by many friends or acquaintances. Some arrived—and survived in our files—on scraps of paper and may therefore be imperfectly worded or attributed. To the authors, contributors and original sources, our thanks, and where appropriate, our apologies. –The Editors

CREDITS

Compiled by: Dan Zadra
Designed by: Sarah Forster & Jessica Phoenix

ISBN: 978-1-932319-88-0

3rd printing. Printed in China with soy inks.

THANK YOU

COMPILED BY DAN ZADRA

DESIGNED BY SARAH FORSTER & JESSICA PHOENIX

COMPENDIUM®
INCORPORATED

ALL THE GREAT BLESSINGS OF MY LIFE
ARE PRESENT IN MY THOUGHTS TODAY.

Phoebe Cary

I awoke this morning with devout
thanksgiving for my friends....

Ralph Waldo Emerson

My heart gives thanks for
empty moments given to dreams,
and for thoughtful people who
help those dreams come true.

William S. Braithwaite

SOME PEOPLE ADD SO MUCH
BEAUTY TO BEING HUMAN.

Kobi Yamada

THERE ARE SOULS IN THIS WORLD
WHO HAVE THE GIFT OF FINDING
JOY EVERYWHERE—AND LEAVING
IT BEHIND THEM WHEN THEY GO.

Frederick William Faber

YOU ARE ONE OF MY
NICEST THOUGHTS.

Georgia O'Keeffe

YOUR PRESENCE
IS A PRESENT TO
THOSE WHO KNOW AND
APPRECIATE YOU.

Unknown

THE WORK OF YOUR HEART, THE
WORK OF TAKING TIME, TO LISTEN,
TO HELP, IS ALSO YOUR GIFT TO
THE WHOLE OF THE WORLD.

Jack Kornfield

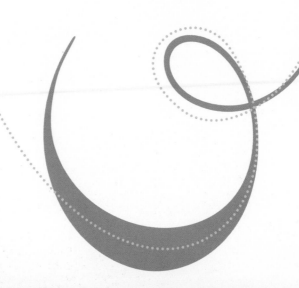

THE GOOD YOU DO IS NOT
LOST THOUGH YOU FORGET IT.

Jiri Masala

WHEN YOU CARE, PEOPLE NOTICE.

Susane Berger

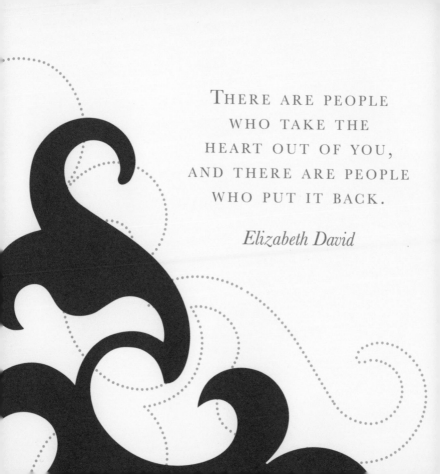

THERE ARE PEOPLE
WHO TAKE THE
HEART OUT OF YOU,
AND THERE ARE PEOPLE
WHO PUT IT BACK.

Elizabeth David

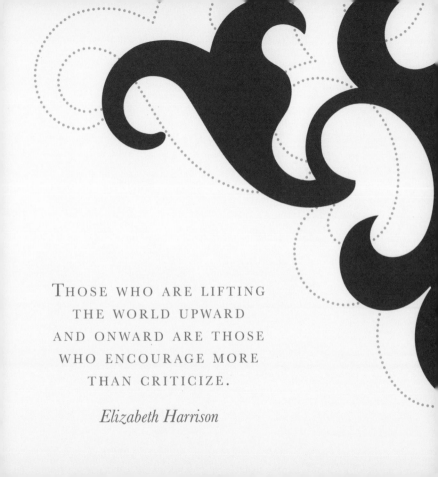

THOSE WHO ARE LIFTING
THE WORLD UPWARD
AND ONWARD ARE THOSE
WHO ENCOURAGE MORE
THAN CRITICIZE.

Elizabeth Harrison

UNSELFISH ACTS ARE THE REAL MIRACLES OUT

WHEN IT COMES TO DOING GOOD THINGS FOR

Dale E. Turner

OF WHICH ALL THE REPORTED MIRACLES GROW.

Ralph Waldo Emerson

OTHERS, SOME PEOPLE WILL STOP AT NOTHING.

THE AFFECT OF ONE
GOOD-HEARTED PERSON
IS INCALCULABLE.

Óscar Arias Sánchez

IF SOMEONE LISTENS, OR STRETCHES
OUT A HAND, OR WHISPERS A KIND WORD
OF ENCOURAGEMENT, OR ATTEMPTS TO
UNDERSTAND, EXTRAORDINARY THINGS
BEGIN TO HAPPEN.

Loretta Girzartis

FEELING GRATITUDE AND NOT EXPRESSING IT IS

LIKE WRAPPING A PRESENT AND NOT GIVING IT.

William Arthur Ward

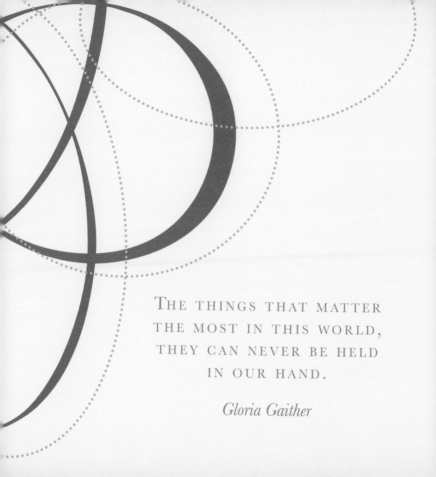

THE THINGS THAT MATTER
THE MOST IN THIS WORLD,
THEY CAN NEVER BE HELD
IN OUR HAND.

Gloria Gaither

TIME HAS A WONDERFUL WAY OF
SHOWING US WHAT REALLY MATTERS.

Margaret Peters

ALL THE STATISTICS IN THE WORLD CAN'T
MEASURE THE WARMTH OF A SMILE.

Chris Hart

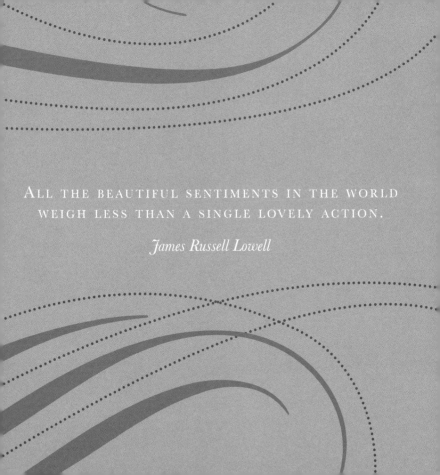

ALL THE BEAUTIFUL SENTIMENTS IN THE WORLD
WEIGH LESS THAN A SINGLE LOVELY ACTION.

James Russell Lowell

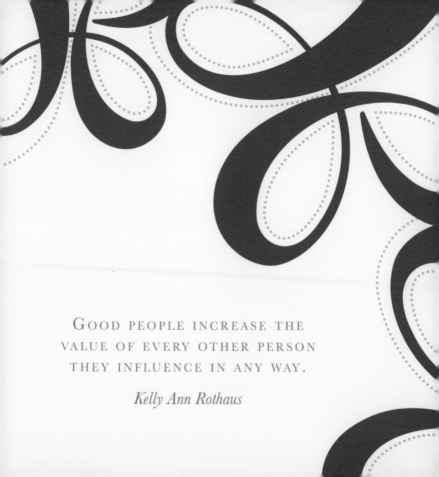

GOOD PEOPLE INCREASE THE
VALUE OF EVERY OTHER PERSON
THEY INFLUENCE IN ANY WAY.

Kelly Ann Rothaus

A TRUE MEASURE OF YOUR WORTH
INCLUDES ALL THE BENEFITS OTHERS
HAVE GAINED FROM YOUR SUCCESS.

Cullen Hightower

A GREAT LIFE IS THE SUM TOTAL
OF ALL THE WORTHWHILE THINGS
YOU'VE BEEN DOING ONE BY ONE.

Richard Bach

THERE IS NO TALLY SHEET IN THE
EXCHANGE OF SMALL KINDNESSES; BUT THERE
IS SHARED MEMORY AND, FROM EACH PERSON,
THE ASSURANCE OF GOOD THINGS TO COME.

Lady Borton

THANK YOU TO ALL THOSE PEOPLE IN
MY LIFE WHO CHANGED IT FOR THE BETTER
BY A WORD, A GIFT, AN EXAMPLE.

Pam Brown

THANK YOU MEANS YOU DIDN'T HAVE TO…
BUT I'M SO GRATEFUL THAT YOU DID.

Chris Gallatin

YOUR HEART HAS
BROUGHT GREAT JOY
TO MANY. THOSE HEARTS
CAN NEVER FORGET YOU.

Flavia Weeden

LOVE AND KINDNESS ARE
NEVER WASTED. THEY ALWAYS
MAKE A DIFFERENCE.

Marian Rogers

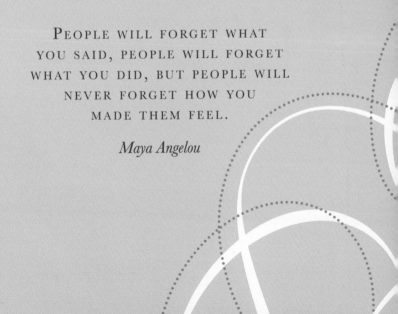

PEOPLE WILL FORGET WHAT
YOU SAID, PEOPLE WILL FORGET
WHAT YOU DID, BUT PEOPLE WILL
NEVER FORGET HOW YOU
MADE THEM FEEL.

Maya Angelou

PEOPLE WHO DEAL WITH LIFE GENEROUSLY
AND LARGE-HEARTEDLY GO ON MULTIPLYING
RELATIONSHIPS TO THE END.

A.C. Benson

WHAT THE HEART GIVES
AWAY IS NEVER GONE. IT IS
KEPT IN THE HEARTS OF OTHERS.

Robin St. John

I WISH YOU ALL THE JOY THAT ONE CAN WISH.

William Shakespeare

MAY HAPPINESS TOUCH YOUR
LIFE TODAY AS WARMLY AS YOU HAVE
TOUCHED THE LIVES OF OTHERS.

Rebecca Forsythe

FOR ALL THAT HAS BEEN, THANKS.
FOR ALL THAT WILL BE, YES.

Dag Hammarskjöld